SANCTIFICATION

*Obtain Spiritual Aptitude &
Unlock Spiritual Authority*

DOROTHY V. MCINTOSH

Divine Works Publishing, LLC.
Royal Palm Beach, Florida USA

© 2024 Dorothy V. McIntosh
SANCTIFICATION: *Obtain Spiritual Aptitude and Unlock Spiritual Authority*

All rights reserved. No part of this publication may be reproduced, stored in a retrieval system, or transmitted in any form or by any means, electronic, mechanical, photocopying, recording or otherwise without the prior permission of the publisher or in accordance with the provisions of the Copyright, Designs, and Patents Act 1988 or under the terms of any license permitting limited copying issued by the Copyright Licensing Agency.

The views expressed in this work are solely those of the author and do not necessarily reflect the views of the publisher, the publisher hereby disclaims any responsibility for them.

ISBN-13: 978-1-949105-62-9 (paperback)
ISBN-13: 978-1-949105-65-0 (hardback)
ISBN-13: 978-1-949105-63-6 (eBook)

First Edition Published: 02/21/2024
Printed in the United States

Divine Works Publishing books are available at special discounts when purchased in quantity for premiums and promotions and for educational and fundraising use. For details, contact: *books@DivineWorksPublishing.com* or call the phone number listed below.

Published by:
Divine Works Publishing, LLC.
Royal Palm Beach, Florida USA
561-990-BOOK (2665)

www.DivineWorksPublishing.com

Dedication

I dedicate this book to the wonderful men and women in the Kingdom of God, reminding you of the extreme urgency to not only teach sanctification but to live a life of sanctification in exclusivity. You are an extraordinary people, gifted and anointed by God to replicate Christ and manifest His glory in the earth realm through righteous living.

I also dedicate this book to the frequently gathered masses whose indulgence may be in the gratification of their flesh through weekly entertainment under the disguise of spiritual worship in the assemblies of God.

May the Lord God of Abraham, Isaac and Jacob encounter you as you enthusiastically enjoy reading this book.

Endorsements

This little book that you hold in your hand, written under the auspices of the Spirit of God afresh, as revelation of the importance; the place and the vitality of the heavenly-ordained process known as sanctification. Sanctification is not merely an emotional, ephemeral, transitory human-ordained process, but rather sanctification for the believer in Christ is a lifetime process.

In many respects according to inspiration, sanctification is as a tender plant that starts out as a mustard seed and grows and develops into a large stable plant. There are many works and a plethora of essays on this topic of sanctification, but for this time and for your soul blessings, you will find that this particular work will bring great comfort and assurance to your soul; in other words it will be as meat in due season sent forth for such a time as this.

Kenneth Major Jr.
Dr. Theology

The word sanctification is most powerful but is not a popular discipline among believers in Christ today. Instead, a life of compromise has become the order of the day and there is very little reverence for God. Many have contravened the required God-ordained life of holiness, therefore the fear of God for many is truly non-existent.

I applaud Dr. Dorothy McIntosh for passionately writing this book on sanctification directly referencing scriptures from the word of God. As I read through the pages I was challenged to examine my own personal walk with the Lord.

I encourage you to read this book with deep reflection and conviction. The application of the daily work of sanctification will transform your life and bring you into true holiness. You have indeed been called and it is God's intent that you be set apart through sanctification to become an effective witness in His kingdom.

Apostle Gaylean Maynard
Resurrection Global Ministries- Jacksonville Fl USA

Table of Contents

Acknowledgments *ix*

Foreword *xi*

I. The Definition of Sanctification *1*

II. The Process of Sanctification *5*

III. The Significance of Sanctification *9*

IV. The Benefits of Sanctification *13*

V. Sanctification Influences Our Perception *23*

VI. The Freedom of Sanctification *27*

VII. Sanctification vs. Sin *39*

VIII. Sanctification Leads to Brokenness *43*

IX. The Altar of Sanctification *47*

About the Author 55

Acknowledgments

Chief Apostle Leon Wallace, a giant of a man in the kingdom, under whose powerful evangelistic ministry I was convicted and accepted Jesus as my personal Savior and Lord. He has truly set the course of my spiritual life and catapulted me to become totally invested in the kingdom of God. Many years ago upon his return to the Bahamas, his message titled "If The Dogs Would Only Bark" has greatly impacted the spiritual leaders of my nation provoking many of them to shift from churchianity to kingdom mindedness. I am grateful and thankful for your contribution, sacrifice, and obedience to God, allowing you to cross my path at that appointed time. *May God's amazing grace be forever yours.*

I also acknowledge a valuable, powerful prophetic voice, a Kingdom Ambassador whom God has sent into my life many years ago. A rare gift to the body of Christ whose deep love and passion for God has truly impacted and transformed my life of prayer. He not only teaches, preaches and demonstrates the word of God, but the evidence of unquestionable manifestations and working of miracles are being realised throughout his ministry. He has directed me to the courtroom of heaven where many victories has and are being won. I greatly appreciate my Father in the Gospel, Apostle Benjamin Nathaniel Smith, Pastor of The Embassy International, Nassau, Bahamas. *God's Ambassador! God's General!*

Additionally, I acknowledge a distinguished, most worthy Ambassador in the Kingdom of Jehovah, whose powerful posture exemplifies the integrity of the gospel. Prophetess Dr. E. Denise Mather, and Invading Force Ministry, has been meticulously instrumental in the transformation of my spiritual stride. Through her humble prophetic guidance I was empowered to flesh out my walk with God and hence live a life of the spiritual discipline of sanctification for the purpose of godliness. I am forever grateful and greatly appreciative for the devoted godly relationship we have shared through the past years. *Thank you Prophetess!*

Foreword

In her book "Sanctification" Dr. Dorothy McIntosh shares profound truths from the Word of God regarding the commandment and requirement of Sanctification in the life of a believer. According to Scripture, sanctification is not an option but a requirement and as mentioned by the author, a pre-condition by God to bring all believers into the fullness of Christ.

Dr. Dorothy provides a clear, concise, and precise definition of sanctification and helps the reader to understand that sanctification *"signifies a life of purity that embodies the spiritual disciplines which are extremely vital to the livelihood of every believer."* I firmly believe every believer needs a reintroduction to the necessity of sanctification as a most fundamental part of our growth and maturity as believers. Too often, as preachers and teachers of the Word of God, we leave out this stage of discipleship in the believer's life. As you read this book, I know that you will be blessed by the 10 Benefits of Sanctification that the author mentions and as well as the process of the Altar of Sanctification.

This is a much needed read and I would dare to say a book that can be used in discipling new converts who are birthed into the Kingdom of God. I was renewed in my heart and spirit and reminded that sanctification is a daily discipline of the believer's life. I know you will be blessed and truly strengthened in your spiritual walk and recommend this book to every believer and commend the author for her "Yes" to God in releasing such great revelatory truths.

Apostle Dr. Brenda Pratt
Senior Pastor, Global Worship Center
National Coordinator Bahamas Manning the Gates

I. The Definition of Sanctification

Sanctification is defined as *the process of being set apart for the special purposes of Jehovah God—and He alone.* It is to separate from a profane to a sacred use, to make oneself holy unto God in all things. It is a thorough cleansing/purging from a sinful nature; fully consecrated unto God. It is a process of spiritual transformation and a complete change within the depths of the heart, mind, and soul. Never is it used in, nor associated with secularism, but is of a far deeper internal state of being separated from worldly lusts, therefore, it can only be used in relation to a Holy God. It is the initiating and sustaining work of Holy Spirit.

One is made sanctified through the blood of Jesus, the Word of God, and Holy Spirit. I Peter 1:2 says,

*"Elect according to the foreknowledge of God the Father,
through sanctification of the Spirit,
unto obedience and sprinkling of the blood of Jesus Christ:"*

Sanctification is the most powerful process of spiritual discipline. If and when one sins, Holy Spirit convicts them immediately. This conviction brings the believer to a point of confession.

The effects of sanctification propels them into a place of true repentance. Once sanctification is in motion, then sin is on the run.

Sanctification therefore, being the disciplinary cleansing instrument for Christ-likeness, must be held at an utmost level. In other words, it must be taken more seriously than the ministerial giftings, which are given without repentance. They are inclusive of the preaching of the word, prophesying, healing, etc.

The Apostle Paul states in I Corinthians 9:16,

"But I keep under my body, and bring it into subjection: lest that by any means, when I have preached to others, I myself should be a castaway."

Furthermore, sanctification should be viewed as a prerequisite in the believers experience. It must be in an order of prominence, meaning that in terms of sequence and importance, the work of sanctification takes prominence and is similar to that of the root of the tree being its establishment and firm foundation.

I. The Definition of Sanctification

Once sanctification is in motion, sin is on the run.

II. The Process of Sanctification

The genesis of the process of sanctification calls for total isolation. This process follows the acceptance of Jesus Christ as your personal Savior and Lord. Frequently, there ought to be times when the believer is undisturbed, uninterrupted, fully immersed with God, soaking in His presence. This sanctifying process is to designed to build a prayer posture, engage the spiritual disciplines of silence and solitude, yield completely to Holy Spirit, and be cleansed daily in mind, heart, body, spirit, and soul. The process of sanctification initiates holy living and infuses spiritual growth in the life of the believer. Over time, a believer progresses to becoming fully cloaked in the fruit of the Spirit, (loving, joyful, peaceable, kind, humble, self controlled).

Additionally, whilst engaged in this work of sanctification these twin components are also inclusive of the spiritual disciplines of fasting and prayer. Jesus went into the wilderness for this purpose, and as we read the account it is clear that this time of fasting and prayer was not just a cursory experience but rather an intense emptying of Himself by this process and at the same time totally relying on the power of God the Father.

The lesson is for us that, like the Master, the servants also must pursue a path, a process of emptying and totally surrendering himself to the will of God. Thus it was, Jesus was fully prepared to meet the tempter, and so shall it be with us. To do otherwise renders the believer vulnerable (defenseless, powerless, weak, unfortified) to the enemy's attacks and hence, defeated. It is quite dangerous for a believer to be found uncovered (exposed) to the hunter of his soul; that wicked serpent whose only intent is to steal, to kill and to destroy; therefore every demonic door (entrance) to our spirit-man must be tightly closed. We must give no place to the enemy. This is the purpose of daily sanctification—to defeat the evil one.

Oftentimes, this sanctifying process may appear to be unbearable but by infinite grace it is not unreachable. As a result of this fiery process one achieves spiritual strength, development, advancement, and empowerment; this brings about spiritual maturity. Through this spiritual cleansing process, one attains spiritual fruitfulness. It involves tolerance and patience which relates to humility, causing the believer to exemplify Christ in his/her lifestyle. Let it be noted that this call, no less by the Master Himself, is to pay special attention to the work of fasting and prayer.

In at least one recorded incident in scripture the Savior gave high recognition to this dual work when he said in Matthew 17:21,

"Howbeit this kind goeth not out but by prayer and fasting.

The process of sanctification greatly contributes to our manifesting the express image of God. Sanctification is as much a command in scripture as the command by Jesus to love one another, therefore, sanctification is a precondition by God to bring all believers into the fullness of Christ.

Sanctification is akin to holiness; it cannot be obtained in a moment of time, but rather is progressive and indeed the work of a lifetime.

> *Sanctification is akin to holiness; it cannot be obtained in a moment of time, but rather is progressive and indeed the work of a lifetime.*

III. The Significance of Sanctification

Sanctification signifies a life of purity which embodies specific spiritual disciplines vital to the livelihood of the believer. It presents an undiluted, distinctive, atmosphere to be worn daily, as a garment of distinction. In other words, sanctification dresses you with the pure presence of God. One must be intentional about being daily outfitted with the garment of sanctification; your very existence becomes adorned with His life and glory and will be visible to others.

The scripture declares in Exodus 34:29-30,

"And it came to pass, when Moses came down from Mount Sinai with the two tables of testimony in Moses' hand, when he came down from the mount, that Moses wist not that the skin of his face shone while he talked with him. And when Aaron and all the children of Israel saw Moses, behold, the skin of his face shone; and they were afraid to come near him."

Being clothed therefore with this garment of sanctification, frees the believer from befoulment and all manner of evil. It is the heavenly detergent that cleanses, purges and keeps you in the way of holiness.

Ephesians 5:26 reads,

> *"That he might sanctify and cleanse it with the washing of water by the word."*

II Timothy 2:21 states,

> *"If a man therefore purge himself from these, he shall be a vessel of honor, sanctified, and meet for the master's use, and prepared unto every good work."*

The prevalence of sanctification in one's life, causes Holy Spirit to anoint, guide, teach and work through that individual, causing him/her to become an instrument in the hand of God. He then uses them in supernatural ways. Sanctification exposes in exhibiting, putting on display the sanctified one.

III. The Significance of Sanctification

Sanctification dresses you with the pure presence of God

IV. The Benefits of Sanctification

A) Word & Truth

It is imperative that readers of the holy book *not* ignore that the word of God is eternally connected, bound up, and wrapped up in the process of sanctification. Therefore, the word of God and the sanctifying process could well be described as the two oars that are needed for a small boat on the lake. Except the two oars are rowing together, the boat can neither go forward or backward, but if one oar is used the result will be spinning and dizziness and a failure to reach a desired haven. I Timothy 4:5 declares,

"For it is sanctified by the word of God and prayer."

So then the word of God and the sanctifying process is inextricably bound for time and eternity.

Did you notice in the aforementioned text that the word of God is the agency that effectuates and both initializes and confirms the ongoing sanctification process? *"Sanctified by the word and prayer."* It is evident that in the neglect of immersing oneself in the rhema word not only neutralizes the sanctification process but renders the seeker spiritually impotent and grossly confused. What

an awesome responsibility then lays on the shoulders of those who are called to be teachers and expounders of the word. In the words of the Savior, *"we are required to eat His flesh,"* "receive nourishment," "drink His blood" (quench one's thirst). It is vital therefore that every true hearted believer with regards to the word settled in his/her heart that this quote unquote word should and must take preeminence over all other words, sayings, dogmas, and any other uninspired proclamation that may be imposed from established religions, long standing institutions or governmental edicts.

Psalms 119:89 reads,

"Forever O Lord Thy word is settled in heaven."

So then whatever we may think or even propose to know if it is not a "thus says the Lord," not only is it not worthy of our consideration, but it should at the earliest possible occasion be dismissed and denigrated. It is encumbered upon every true genuine christian believer to not only promote but to demonstrate in his/her life that the word of God is the substance on which he is to feed and to be sustained.

This fact is illustrated in the voice of many of God's ancient prophets. Here the weeping prophet,

"Thy words were found and I did eat them;
and thy word was unto me the joy and rejoicing of mine heart:
for I am called by thy name, Lord God of hosts."
-Jeremiah 15:16.

Every child of God shall forever find joy, satisfaction and total fulfillment from feasting in the word of God. As for Ezekiel, God's ancient watchman on the wall, the ancient seer tells us that the word of God was as sweet as honey in his mouth, like him we too are commanded to eat "this/ this word." Ezekiel 3:3. It is as much a command for us today as it was for Ezekiel in his day to fill our bellies with His words and without a shadow of a doubt we too will exclaim that the word of the Lord is as sweet as honey in our mouth. It would be remiss not to draw attention to that long-suffering extremely patient patriot name Job who declared even in the midst of severe trials and tribulations,

> *"I have esteemed the words of His mouth*
> *more than my necessary food,"*
> *-Job 23:12*

In other words for Job and likewise for us, if we have to make a choice between the word of God and our necessary food, quote unquote give me the bible.

Finally when He who was given to be the propitiation for our sins whilst engaging in an existential battle with the prince of darkness, He left on record for all mankind to know that every decision we are called upon to make we must give the highest consideration to what the word of God says.

Give ear to the Savior's command,

> *"Man shall not live by bread alone;*
> *but by every word that proceedeth*
> *out of the mouth of God."*
> *-Matthew 4:4.*

Focus for a minute on the word *every*, it doesn't mean some, it doesn't mean a selected portion but it means just what it says, every word of God. The word of God then must be our guide book, our chart, our compass, our sword, our food, our drink, our lamp and our joy. Little wonder then that the psalmist declared,

> *"For thou hast magnified thy word above all thy name."*
> *-Psalm 138:2b*

Truth is like a refiner's fire. It is designed to unearth our nakedness, root out lusts from our hearts, and outfit us in righteousness. Jesus prayed to His Father in the book of St. John 17:17,

"Sanctify them through Thy truth; for Thy word is truth."

Here the Savior tells us plainly that the work of sanctification cannot be accomplished/achieved apart from the power in the word of God. Hence the statement through the words that I speak,

*"It is the Spirit that quickeneth,
the flesh profiteth nothing, the words that I speak unto you,
they are Spirit, and they are life." -John 6:63*

Our Savior was the embodiment of truth. When inquired of, concerning His directions and movements by the Apostle Thomas, He responded *"...I am… I am the way, the Truth…"*

If ever one would need to handle the truth, see the truth, hear the truth, we need to look no further than to look upon the essence of truth, Jesus Christ the Son of the living God.

B) Purity & Love

Purification is indeed a developmental process that moves the believer along an upward pursuit. Apostle Peter admonishes us to be assiduous in this walk of purity. **"And beside this, giving all diligence, add to your faith virtue.; and to virtue knowledge; and to knowledge temperance; and to temperance patience; and to patience godliness; and to godliness brotherly kindness; and to brotherly kindness charity (love). For if these things be in you, and abound, they make you that ye shall neither be barren nor unfruitful in the knowledge of our Lord Jesus Christ" -II Peter 1:5-8.**

It is therefore important that believers attain and maintain purity in spirit; for it is the central merit of our spiritual existence.

The bible says, *"Unto the pure all things are pure."* Titus 1:15a. Purity begins at home, that is, in the mind of the individual. In Philippians 4:8, the seasoned Apostle Paul told us to think (meditate) on the things that are pure. The believer must embody the spiritual element of purity to live life to the fullest esteem, in soberness, peacefulness and godliness. Purity encompasses the heart, the mind, the spirit and the body. None can be pure without the other. In other words, if one becomes defiled, it is at the expense of all the others.

"But unto them that are defiled and unbelieving is nothing pure; but even their mind and conscience is defiled." -Titus 1:15^b

This is why sanctification is a daily undertaking, so that the life of the believer remains on the pathway of purity.

"He (Jesus) gave Himself for us that He might redeem us from all iniquity and purify unto Himself a peculiar people, zealous of good works." -Titus 2:14

A pure heart constitutes a heart of love. Purity of spirit means purity of life. In our daily press for sanctification we ought to be mindful to incorporate the words of the Prophet David in **Psalm 51:10, "Create in me a clean (pure) heart O God; and renew a right spirit within me."** This is the only way one can love in truth. *Sanctification + Purity + Holiness = Godliness!*

Love is not selfish or shamefaced, never reluctant to do what is right. It is not hot-tempered nor is it ill-mannered; but love is patient; love is kind; love is humble all of the time. It is not easily provoked; it doesn't envy; holds no grudge; it is not jealous; it knows no malice; but love is truly the essence of Christ; therefore, love is the more excellent way.

C) Power & Boldness

Through sanctification, the child of God will be quickened with the manifested power of God which the early church possessed. It will be demonstrated with great authority and boldness. The Apostle Peter declared in **Acts 4:31, "And when they prayed, the place was shaken where they were assembled together; and they were all filled with the Holy Ghost, and they spake the word of God with boldness."**

Sanctification therefore, makes this unlimited power available to all who obediently yield themselves to Christ's commands. Obedience is the prerequisite to receiving Power. Jesus' instructions to His apostles was to tarry in Jerusalem and wait for the promise of the Father. They simply obeyed and were endued with power placed upon them by the Holy Spirit, hence, proclaimed the word of God with great boldness.

Submitting to the spiritual disciplines of prayer, fasting, intake of the word of God, worship, praise, silence and solitude, causes one to receive a wellspring of divine revelation giving them boldness to discharge the word of God in truth, without hesitation, even in the midst of unfavorable circumstances. The bible says that, *"the righteous are bold as a lion." -Proverbs28:1*[b]

D) Meekness & Fear

I Peter 3:15 declares,

> *"But sanctify the Lord God in your hearts:*
> *and be ready always to give an answer*
> *to every man that asketh you a reason of the hope*
> *that is in you with meekness and fear:"*

To buttress this claim that sanctification produces meekness, we need not cite any other example than that of Israel's greatest military general, lawgiver, prophet and the last Melchizedek priest other than Moses himself. The Creator Himself testifies that Moses {though he was a great man} was the meekest man on the earth. *Numbers 12:3 reads,*

> *"Now the man Moses was very meek, above all the men which were upon the face of the earth."*

We here see, through definite and clear examples, the humility that characterized the life of Moses as a servant of the Most High and as a lover of the people of God.

Example 1

When Jethro the priest of Midian and father-in-law of Moses brought his wife and children after they departed from Egypt, Jethro was invited by Moses to spend some time with them. The scripture points out to us that on the second day of the visit, Jethro observed Moses' taxing and challenging administrative duties and suggested to Moses that if he were to continue in this way, in a short while both he and the entire congregation of Israel would end up stressed out, confused and disorganized. He went on to further suggest that Moses would take heed to his (Jethro's) simple but logical executive plan. Though Moses was a chosen visible leader of the Hebrews, yet as a result of his level of sanctification, he humbled himself and willingly accepted the advice of his father-in-law.

Example 2

On one occasion after spending forty days in communing with Jehovah, Moses returned to the camp and was totally unaware that as a result of the glory of God shining on his face was to pose a problem to his people. The record says that when Aaron and the leaders saw Moses they were speechless and terrified and literally withdrew themselves from him. When Moses inquired as to why, all they could do was indicate by pointing that something was "wrong" with his face. Moses learned that the glory which shone from his face was a reflection of the glory of God. This sanctified yet humble leader requested that a veil be brought forth so as to cover his face whenever he was to speak to the leaders and people. And so it was whenever Moses went to commune with God, on his return he veiled his face. Let it be settled therefore, that a key manifested component of the sanctifying process is a manifestation of humility or meekness. (Exodus 34:29-34). We must radiate Christ.

E) Faith & Unity

Faith is the spiritual substance of that which is to be and once action is initiated, reality surfaces. It is the active ingredient that comes with sanctification. Sanctification whips up faith. Trying to be faithful outside of sanctification is like trying to swim in a desert.

Think about it.

We understand from the written word of God that the Sanctifier of our lives is indeed the author and the finisher of our faith; therefore the process of faith is most unusual. Absolute trust and dependency must be placed in and upon Him. Faith is our guide to living the purposeful life He has intended for us. It is the main route or freeway or channel between us and God. When we are not vigilant in our faith we tend to doubt the capabilities of God. Faith in God not only gives us hope for this life but prepares us for eternity in time; meaning that in this life we look forward by faith to that day which can be any day where we will endlessly be beyond the tomb. And so it is imperative that we use keen faith to the fullest capacity to gain access to His Supernatural power, hence, fulfill His purpose in our lives. Lack of faith cripples our life's journey. With faith intact there's no wondering of the mind.

II Corinthians 5:7 reads,

"For we walk by faith, not by sight."

So then faith is undeniably the premise of our walk with God. The powerpack agreement of faith and unity supported by prayer, will fortify relationships, break down walls, loose the bands of wickedness, undo the heavy burdens and let the oppressed go free. Having unity is powerful. It brings wholeness to the life of the believer whether it involves natural, spiritual and or ministerial relationships. It is a state of dwelling, a position of being glued together by a decision or decisions and accomplishing one's goals.

Psalms 133:12a states,

> *"How good and how pleasant it is*
> *for brethren to dwell together in unity!*
> *It is like precious ointment upon the head…"*

In an attempt to build the tower of Babel to reach up to heaven, the people had one mindset and were well on their way to accomplish their goal. It took the divine intervention of the Almighty to confuse their language and bring to a halt their unifying league.

F) Exclusivity

By its very definition, sanctification carries with it the connotation of separateness or apartness. It is almost impossible to conjure up in one's mind the thought of being sanctified apart from being exclusive. The sanctified believer then will demonstrate to all that his life, his purposes and his conversations is dedicated exclusively to the work of God and to the mission of Christ. It is only reasonable then to expect that the sanctified life is a life of exclusivity. As there is only one God, one Lord and one Father of us all (three in one), so too, the sanctified believer must give himself totally (body, soul and spirit) his all in all.

Sanctification + Purity + Holiness = Godliness!

V. Sanctification Influences Our Perception

The work of sanctification is in essence a multilateral operation. In other words the process of sanctification impacts every aspect of the believers life. For example, sanctification has a bearing on one's social, mental and emotional, spiritual, psychological and one's total perspective on life. We can say with surety that true sanctification brings total transformation. Hence, the scriptures teach that there is no such thing as partial sanctification or sometimes sanctification or post sanctification. There is no category for an ex-sanctified believer. Sanctification empowers the believer to perceive, that is to see things differently.

The sanctified perception therefore is freed from suspicion, mistrust and or distrust, and is rather clear in its views and visions.

Contrary to this is the innate fully human views and perspective on life. It is natural therefore for the unsanctified mind to be filled with unsanctified questions and quibblings concerning the issues of life. Such a mindset makes mountains out of mold-hill, makes a tempest in a teapot and sees a lion behind every tree. Conversely, the sanctified perspective promotes peace and quietude because you know who you are and whose you are. As a result of this

process of sanctification the believer then has no other recourse, but to see his brother and or his sister as an equal to himself. In truth he cannot do otherwise.

> *"No man is an island, no man stands alone, Each man's joy is joy to me, each man's grief is my own. We need one another, so I will defend, each man as my brother, each man as my friend."*
> -Written by John Donne.

V. Sanctification Influences Our Perception

> *Sanctification has a bearing on one's social, mental and emotional, spiritual, psychological and one's total perspective on life*
>
>

VI. The Freedom of Sanctification

In Jesus' own words recorded in St. John 8:32, "Ye shall know the truth, and the truth shall make you free." It is curious to know that our Savior chooses His words most deliberately in this text. Our Lord did not say that the truth will set us free as is often quoted. And why not you may ask, simply because the word "set" carries with it the meaning of settling, settlement or completion. For example, **Psalm 119:89 declares, "Forever Oh Lord Thy word is settled in heaven."** This word *settle,* every mason could well comprehend that when working with concrete or mortar once it settles it hardens and is therefore very difficult to break up or remove. Our Savior in this text chooses the word "make" as to apply a continuing process. Thus it is with the truth that we have many things to learn about the truth and many many more things to unlearn that we thought were true.

God's intent is that sanctification become innate to the believer's way of life so that the enslavement of sin be demolished. When the word of truth is intertwined in the believer's daily lifestyle, the light of sanctification shines forth and dispels every nook of darkness. **"Now the Lord is that Spirit, and where the Spirit of the Lord is, there is freedom"- II Corinthians 3:17.** It is in knowing and obeying the truth of God's word that makes one free.

Your Body - His Temple

I Corinthians 6:19 -20 says,

"What? Know ye not that your body is the temple of the Holy Ghost which is in you, which ye have of God, and ye are not your own? For ye are bought with a price: therefore glorify God in your body, and in your spirit, which are God's."

Do you know that Holy Spirit resides within you? Yes, your body is His house-His dwelling place. How do you treat His temple? Do you sanitize (sanctify) His temple on a day to day basis? If not, then why not? You profess Him as Lord and Saviour of your life, therefore, it is required that you be daily sanitized with the word of God and perfumed with prayer. Consider for a moment the daily rounds of the Levitical priests, and consider also that the Apostle declares that every believer belongs to the royal priesthood of Christ. Further, consider this that before the priest began his ceremonial duties he had to be washed, cleansed and if you please sanitized before going into the holy place. In other words God would teach His people that when approaching the Most High, not only their minds were to be pure but their bodies also were to be cleansed.

A perfect illustration of this is recorded in the book of Exodus 19:10, 14, hear the words of the eternal,

"And the Lord said unto Moses, Go unto the people, and sanctify them today and tomorrow, and let them wash their clothes." "And Moses went down from the mount unto the people, and sanctified the people; and they washed their clothes."

Are you disciplined with the right diet that is beneficial to the body? In the Levitical law, there are instructions of the foods you should abstain from putting into God's temple. This law has not been abolished, it still stands today. The purpose is to maintain excellent health so there be no delay or deterrence or cancellation of your spiritual assignments. God, even today, speaks directly to His servants instructing them to abstain from specific diets that negatively affect their health, causing illnesses and weakness (deterioration) of the body, hence the mind and the spirit.

It is for this reason that Apostle Paul gives a strong admonition to every present truth believer, "whether ye eat, or drink, or whatever ye do, do all to the glory of God." To put in modern terms or in the language for millennials the Apostle Paul will have us to know that whatever involves our bodies, whether it is eating foods or drinking liquid or any activity that involves the body/temple, if its not to the glory and honor of God we should desist/leave it alone. And it is for this reason that the business of temperance is closely aligned to the work of sanctification. Thus it was that Moses exercised temperance. Thus it was that Elijah exercised temperance, and John the Baptizer and ultimately Jesus Himself in the wilderness of temptation. The scriptures give ample references where God required (and He still does now) that His people be fully cognizant in keeping their body-temples holy/ sanctified to the honor and glory of His name. It has always been God's desire to dwell in the hearts of His people, that is why we have on record,

> *"And let them make me a sanctuary;*
> *that I may dwell among them."*
> *-Exodus 25:8.*

When the time came the portable sanctuary in the wilderness evolved into Solomon's temple. But the Most High desired a closer, yes a more intimate relationship with each believer, yes even to dwell in their hearts, in their body-temples. With this knowledge we are expected to ensure that whatever we put into our temples or on our temples would be accepted by the Father without question.

This matter of temple attire and temple nourishment was and still is most important to the God of Abraham, Isaac and Jacob. How so you may ask? Please note that shortly after delivering His people from Egypt the Most High started a dialog with them concerning their diet. On one hand the people wanted what we would call today, Kentucky and Burger King, "the fleshpot of Egypt." Exodus 16:3. On the other hand the Lord wanted to give them a diet that was suitable for their wilderness travel, manna from heaven. And after a terrible experience of food poisoning and death the Hebrews ate manna for forty years, no belly ache, no heart ache, no diabetes, no hypertension, no doctors, no hospitals, and the bible says, not even their feet was swollen. Thus the diet was suitable for their bodies/temples and their climate. Further Jehovah would have them to know that when they were to enter the promised land they were to maintain their health by avoiding certain dietary food items. The entire eleven chapters of Leviticus is particularly detailed as to what is acceptable to God for food. Although some would believe today that these dietary permissions and restrictions are antiquated, the New Testament scriptures clearly teach otherwise. In Acts 15:20, the Apostle James gives clear evidence that even after the death of Christ these health laws (concerning meats and blood was still enforced and binding).

"But that we write unto them,
that they abstain from pollutions of idols, and from fornication,
and from things strangled, and from blood."

Hence, at the close of his apostolic ministry, the beloved apostle John in his third epistle through the saints of God, would make mention of his earnest dual desires for God's people then and through the ages to come here his plea,

"Beloved, I wish above all things that thou mayest prosper
and be in health, even as thy soul prospereth."
-III John:2

Let us consider a little more carefully the shared-weight of the words here penned, "I wish," meaning "I desire," "it is my best hope for you," "let it be." In other words if I were to bequeath to you my final will and testament it would be this "above all things," that whatever you do in the final analyses above all things that you be in health even as your soul prospers.

The Apostle Paul says in **I Corinthians 3:16, "Know ye not that ye are the temple of God, and that the Spirit of God dwelleth in you?"** How reserved are you in the way you present God's temple in public? Are we not instructed to present our bodies as living sacrifices holy and acceptable unto God? Romans 12:1. Are you flamboyant, loose or immodest? How are your thought patterns, are they intact or chaotic? Are we not commanded to in so far as our thought patterns are concerned to let our minds be like that of Christ's? According to **Philippians 2:5 "Let this mind be in you, which was also in Christ Jesus."**

It is firmly established in the scriptures that the Holy Spirit is more than an electrical or magnetic force or some invisible intangible motorized phenomenon. Just a cursory examination of the bible proves to us that the Holy Spirit of God is equal to the Father and the Son in essence, in power, in nature and in person and yet they are three distinct personalities in one person. Take for example Peter's interview with Ananias in chapter five of Acts. Peter declares that Ananias didn't lie to him as an apostle but lied to the Holy Spirit. Ask yourself this question: is it possible to lie or communicate through an electrical force? Can you command electricity to start or to cease from flowing? Can you invite magnetic or electrical force into your person by simply asking? Furthermore, think this through, we are educated by the apostle Paul to "grieve not the Holy Spirit." It has never been recorded nor will it ever be recorded some person or individual has been reported as grieving an electrical, magnetic or natural force. Let it be forever settled in our hearts that the Spirit of God is the very One sent to be the Comforter/ Paraclete from the

Father.

He is also the One who is doing the ministry of intercession on behalf of the children of God. Here is what the apostle Paul said in **Romans 8:26 "Likewise the Spirit also helpeth our infirmities: for we know not what we should pray for as we ought; but the Spirit Himself maketh intercession for us with groanings that cannot be uttered."** Let us forever be careful not to allow the spirit of the wicked one to confuse or confound us on this matter for we all know that he is a deceiving spirit but God has given us the Spirit of truth. As we have been told that all the books of the bible meet and end in the book of revelation. It is there that we should expect to find a clear and resounding call from the living spirit of God.

There are at least seven calls by the Spirit of God Himself throughout the age of the church since apostolic times. We find the Spirit in His admonition to each section of the church "to hear what the spirit says unto the church." As expected, in the very final chapter and the very final book of the bible, in the final section of that chapter, comes the loving call "And the Spirit and the bride say, Come. And let him that heareth say, Come. And let him that is a thirst come. And whosoever will, let him take the water of life freely." And so we see the full, complete and perfect will of God demonstrated in the divine activity of the spirit. How so one may ask, look at the first chapter of the book of revelation, it begins with the spirit of God and ends with the spirit of God.

Hear the testimony of the aged apostle, "I was in the spirit on the Lord's day." Revelation 1:10. And his second encounter was found in Revelation chapter 4:2. The Holy Spirit is the third in command of the Godhead. When Jesus spoke with His disciples in St. John 14:16-17, He said,

"And I will pray the Father, and He shall give you another Comforter, that he may abide with you forever; Even the Spirit of truth; whom the world cannot receive, because it seeth Him not, neither knoweth Him: but ye know Him for He dwelleth with you,

and shall be in you." Jesus Christ - Our Sanctifier

It is important that we fully grasp this concept, "He that sanctifies is also He that separates/consecrates." In other words the Sanctifier is also the *Consecrator*. This truth is forcibly set forth in the experience of the children of Israel in their blatant apostasy at the foot of Mount Sinai. On his return from receiving the royal law, the scripture declares that Moses' anger was "waxed hot" and he was commanded by God to call forth a separation/consecration of all those who were on the Lord's side. Exodus 32:26-29. This then would be the first established call in scripture for the sons of Levi to receive the ordination of ministry.

Further on, Jehovah would establish a further separation/ consecration/ sanctification of the children of Aaron from the Levitical tribe. So while the priesthood was given to the family of Aaron only, the entire tribe of Levi was dedicated to the work of ministry. Again while all priests were Levites not every Levite was a priest. These words are fraught with power as we investigate further this commandment given to Moses, "and thou shall sanctify them," meaning set them apart for holy use only or in modern language to be used only for the purpose it is dedicated to. To use that thing or that article in any way otherwise than it was designed would be a violation of the plain expressed instruction of Jehovah and will produce nothing but corruption, contamination and confusion. "That they may be most holy." In other words they may be used at all times and in every way only for the purposes for which they have been designated and dedicated. To be used otherwise would result in desecration.

Clearly the concept of sanctifying cannot be separated or divorced from the concept of consecration, dedication, commitment and total devotion. From just a cursory examination of the following verses will show clearly a sure foundation to this concept.

In Exodus 30:29, Moses was instructed in preparation of the sanctuary where the people of God were to meet and worship

Jehovah to set apart/ sanctify/ consecrate various article of furniture, priestly attire, an altar of sacrifice, and the priests to do the work of ministering between God and man. **"And thou shall sanctify them, that they may be most holy: whatsoever toucheth them shall be holy."** The Sanctifier our Lord and Savior Jesus Christ has from the very beginning by our God and His Father has been commissioned to initiate the work of sanctification, separation and consecration. We know this because the scripture in both the gospel of Luke and the book of Revelation would have us to know that in the ions of eternity past according to the book of Revelation, there was war in heaven. This then would be the first account in the history of the universe of God where there was a separation for those who were on the Lord's side and those who were on the side of the enemy of God.

Is there little wonder then that even today the process of consecrating, separating, sanctifying continues. Each child of God is called upon to examine himself not just to see if he's in the faith but also to determine his degree of sanctification, separation, consecration unto God. This work is not a suggestion or mere consideration but our Lord Himself requires it of all of His children. In this way, we can better appreciate that oft quoted statement that true sanctification is the work of a lifetime. So contrary to the false notion of so many "christian believers," that the act or process of sanctification is a momentary fleeting occasional experience that could be turned off and on like a light switch, we see with clear vision that sanctification is not a once and for all activity but rather, again, an ongoing process.

Take note that this business of sanctification is a requirement of all who are planning to or ever to enter into the eternal glories. At different points in the scriptures the Lord has left for His people, on record what He means for us to understand about "heavenly requirements."

Here are a few references from the scriptures, *Deuteronomy 10:12, "And now, Israel, what doth the Lord thy God require of thee, but to fear the Lord thy God, to walk in all his ways, and to love him, and to serve the Lord thy God with all thy heart and with all thy soul."* Can we not see in this call that God is requiring us to offer/ present/ dedicate/ consecrate and commit ourselves entirely to Him - mind, body and soul. Very often many believers are more than willing to offer up their bodies and souls, but are challenged to give their minds completely. Inspiration also admonishes us that there ought to be a renewing of our minds continuously. Romans 12:2.

Further, no less a person than the wise man himself informs us that we ought to guard well the affections of the heart/mind, for out of the heart flows the issues of life. Proverbs 4:23. This is also true according to one noted philosopher, "man is not what he thinks he is, but what he thinks, he is."

Micah 6:8,

"He hath shewed thee, O man, what is good and what doth the Lord require of thee, but to do justly, and to love mercy, and to walk humbly with thy God.

The prophet Micah in response to five profound and challenging questions has left on record for the people of God for all times what it is that the God of heaven requires of us all. This is not a sub-position but note well in answer to the questions the prophet declared emphatically *"he hath shown thee O man what is good."* In other words there's no need to wonder, no need for further queries. The Lord tells us definitely what it is that He would have us do which are valuable and acceptable in His sight. Here they are:

1. "Do justly." We are not required to think justly or to write "justly" or even to speak justly, but the requirement says plainly to do justly. So when we know better God expects, yea, requires of us to do better. Remember the admonition of the Apostle James when he calls on us to be "doers of the word and not hearers only."

2. "Love mercy." The popular adage says, "when you're powerful be merciful." Oh that every believer would incorporate this grace in their intercourse with their fellow believers and others

generally. The Lord himself makes an invitation in the beatitudes to practice this gift of mercy when he said, "Blessed are the merciful for they shall obtain mercy." Matthew 5:7. Mercy is that attribute of God which causes him to send rain on the just and the unjust and causes the sun to shine on the good, the bad, and the ugly.

    3. "And to walk humbly with thy God." Humility is that godly trait that all who will enter the pearly gates must be completely immersed in. For humility/meekness is required for all to inherit the future new earth.

> *"Blessed are the meek for they shall inherit the earth."*
> *Matthew 5:5.*

    Finally consider this the direct opposite characteristic of humility is (and we all know this) pride.
I Corinthians 4:2,

> *"Moreover it is required in stewards,*
> *that a man be found faithful."*

    Here we are informed that the Lord of glory considers us as believers to be stewards of his household, of all his goods. Have you ever considered yourself to be a steward of God? If so, note well that it is required of stewards to be found faithful *in all things, at all times,* and *in all places.* The truth is while many may consider themselves to be committed, sadly they lack faithfulness. Likewise while there are some who are strong for the things of God, yet they are deficient in faithfulness. Faithfulness is as indispensable to stewardship as heat is to light.

    In summary when something is required it is indispensable, in other words we cannot do without that thing. Thus we can conclude that sanctification is an indispensable article necessary for salvation; in other words there is no such thing as an unsanctified believer or bible practitioner.

VI. The Freedom of Sanctification

Mercy is that attribute of God which causes him to send rain on the just and the unjust and causes the sun to shine on the good, the bad, and the ugly.

VII. Sanctification vs. Sin

Believer's are to obey the commanding word of God allowing the inner work of sanctification to manifest on the outside. As we develop a closer relationship with God through the fire of sanctification, those dark areas of sin in our lives are relinquished.

Sanctification institutes Christ-likeness and shields the believer from sin. The premise of your sanctification is based on *Colossians 3:9-10,*

"Lie not one to another, seeing that ye have put off the old man with his deeds; And have put on the new man, which is renewed in knowledge after the image of him that created him."

How often we fail to appreciate the gravity of these verses stated here in Colossians. It bears noting that the first instruction that the Apostle gives here is the business of lying *not* one to another. Obviously in this text the Apostle will have us to understand that the first and greatest enemy through the process of sanctification is the matter of falsifying/lying in our words. Think about it, what was the first sin? Was it not believing a lie? The serpent lied to the woman "ye shall not surely die" and the history of the world proves that from

that very first lie to the very present time many lives are based on lies and falsehood. Thus we are admonished to not only lie not one to another, but to speak the truth in love.

> *"Instead, speaking the truth in love,*
> *we will grow to become in every respect*
> *the mature body of him who is the head,*
> *that is, Christ"*
> *-Ephesians 4:15*

The phrase "speak the truth in love" means speaking what is doctrinally correct and coming from a biblically committed life to someone who needs correction. It's about more than just encouraging honesty, and rather a rich experience of the new way of life that Jesus offers.

What does Scripture say about true love?
What is the love truth in 1 Corinthians 13?
What does speaking the truth in love mean in the Bible?
Ask a follow up...

With sanctification in motion, your gifts and callings are initiated by Holy Spirit. We are called to pursue holiness-sanctification by presenting our members as instruments of righteousness. This is the primary pursuit of the believer's life.

The lack of sanctification is the causation of sin reigning in our mortal bodies, hence, crippling our forward movement in God.

As a believer, if you are not growing, sanctification is not happening. The lack of sanctification equals a lack of godly character, hence making you a danger to yourself and others.

Once sanctification begins, sin is on the run. Sin cannot dwell in the holiness of God.

VII. Sanctification vs. Sin

The lack of sanctification equals a lack of godly character, hence making you a danger to yourself and others.

VIII. Sanctification Leads to Brokenness

When you pursue sanctification, it drives you to a place of brokenness. It is in this place that your whole being becomes vulnerable and submitted to Holy Spirit. It is a place of absolute penitence, full surrender and being broken in your worship unto God. Once totally yielded on the altar of God, your old wineskin is exchanged for new wineskin. Far too many fail to recognize, appreciate or value the scriptural significance of the symbol of the altar. Throughout the old testament and clearly throughout the new testament the altar is represented as a place of and for revival and reformation. In other words, a place of change. It was after the worship of Abel at the altar of sacrifice that we are told that God accepted his offering and commended him. And ever since the time of Noah in Genesis chapter nine, Abraham Genesis 14, and Jacob, the altar was seen as a place of brokenness, repentance, revival and reformation. Throughout the scripture whenever the people of God were in trouble or facing some calamity, they knew where to go and what was required of them. Through powerful and clear examples that are left on record for us in this regard is the experience of Jacob as recorded in Genesis 35:1-4 and the experience of the children of Israel in I Samuel 7:1-10.

Doubtless, every reader of the new testament is more than familiar with the Apostle Paul's longing admonition that is found in **Romans 12:1,**

"I beseech you therefore brethren by the mercies of God that you present your bodies a living sacrifice, holy acceptable unto God which is your reasonable service."

Unlike the previous two mentioned altars and sacrificing, the new testament believer is to present himself as a living sacrifice on the altar of God.

There, your tattered garment will be replaced with the robe of righteousness and the fresh oil of anointing begin to overflow in your life. Take note, that the oil could not flow out of Mary's alabaster box until it was broken.

Regarding this spirit of brokenness, the scriptures supply us with at least three clear cut illustrations of how this brokenness is to be experienced. The prophet Isaiah vividly and with painful utterance declared his brokenness in the presence of the Most High God when he cried out in a mournful tune, *"woe is me! For I am undone; because I am a man of unclean lips, for mine eyes have seen the King, the Lord of hosts."*

When the Lord presented Himself to Daniel in the glory of His power, Daniel exclaimed, *"my comeliness was turned into corruption."*

Our third illustration is seen in the encounter of Peter with our Savior. After a night of toiling without any catch, the Savior bid the fisherman to cast his net on the right side and to his surprise the net was full to a breaking point and the disciples were forced to call out for help from his partners James and John. The latter having secured the catch, Peter, according to the account, rushed unto the beach side, prostrated himself before the Savior, *"depart from me for I am a sinful man."* Luke 5:8. It's important to note also the position of how these three illustrated men found themselves in this state of

brokenness. As for Isaiah, he informs us that he was in the temple, no doubt praying and soliciting the grace and the power of God when the Most High showed up and Isaiah said that His train filled the temple. The account also details for us that Daniel was not just on his knees but also on his face, prostrated before the infinite One. And Luke the physician records that Peter "fell down at Jesus' knees." How then can we deny that with the Most High the act of reverence is more than an indicative, it is an imperative. Thus the prophet
Habakkuk 2:20 said,

*"But the Lord is in His holy temple:
let all the earth keep silence before Him."*

The lesson is that sanctification produces, and is immersed in reverence, hence it is impossible to practice sanctification apart from appreciating the reverence of the Most High.

> And ever since the time of Noah in Genesis chapter nine, Abraham Genesis 14, and Jacob, the altar was seen as a place of brokenness, repentance, revival, and reformation.

IX. The Altar of Sanctification

The call to the altar of sanctification is far beyond self. By this we mean to say, as the apostle Paul admonishes, the altar of sanctification demands of the believer that he or she *"presents their bodies as living sacrifices."* Reinforcing the understanding that every altar demands a sacrifice of some kind. Whether it is a grain, as in the case of the wave sheaf or an offering of wave loaves, or ultimately a lamb, a fowl or a bullock, we must understand that sacrifice takes much spiritual discipline.

This is a call for the believer to be totally, completely, unhesitatingly consecrated to the service of God. In so doing, we give God our hands, our feet our heads, our total selves; not for a moment in time, but a moment by moment (in time) commitment. Let us remember that the God of heaven and earth requires nothing less.

At this altar of sanctification a partial or incomplete offering, a corrupt or blemish offering an insincere and doubtful offering would, by no means, be accepted by Him who reads the thoughts and intents of the heart. God wants it all or nothing at all.

Far too often it would appear that we fail to remember that we have been given a mandate to reach our communities, our nation and by far the nations of the world. But how can we fulfill this heaven ordained mandate without the empowerment promised by the

 SANCTIFICATION: *The Believer's Lifestyle*

Savior **"when He the Spirit of truth is come, He will guide you into all truth"** -John 16:13.

My beloved brothers and sisters this is not only a promise but this is a divine principle.

The spirit of God will not reside in an unconsecrated unsanctified vessel. This is clearly stated by the apostle Peter in Acts chapter 5, *"the Holy Spirit is given unto them that obey Him."* In other words, sanctification—available for all at the altar of sanctification, —comes with a price tag, obedience. Therefore, our altar for the Lord must be garnished with sanctification and must be provided with a lifestyle of obedience and substantial sacrifices. This "sacrifice," is the sacrifice of the flesh, this self-willed spirit, the spirit of pride, hubris, presumptuousness, and self conceit.

At this altar of sanctification we are required to "lay aside every weight and the sin which so easily besets us so that we might run this race with patience." At this altar of sanctification we are commanded to take up our weapons of warfare not of a carnal nature but spiritual weapons which we are to engage and successfully defeat the enemy of our souls. Yes every believer knows that the weapons of our warfare are not carnal but spiritual to the pulling down of strongholds. This altar of sanctification is not necessarily a physical one as it was in the days of the ancient patriarchs. Abraham was known as a worshiper of the true God who made heaven and earth. All who knew Abraham knew him to be a monotheist and he was known to set up his altar as he moved throughout the land of promise. His son Isaac followed the same pattern. Jacob also called Israel never forgot this heaven ordained practice left to him by his grandfather. And even though they all constructed by their own hands their altars of sanctification, yet in their innermost heart, yea even in the recesses of their hearts they established the altar of sanctification. Let us consider a little further this altar of sanctification. Though it is in many respects a physical visible structure as mentioned above it does not necessarily have to be such. The altar calls us to it and we come to the altar of sanctification. It calls us. Note too, that we are to draw near to the altar, the altar does not draw near to us. The altar then is that representation of our desire to come into a closer connection to the God of heaven and we come in a humble, teachable, quiet, seeking spirit with a mindset to always be willing to say, thy will be done, my will be done away with. Although today we are not required to establish a physical altar of sanctification, our innermost being ought to live in the presence of a holy God—without spot without wrinkle, without blemish, or any such thing.

The altar is an exclusive place where God reveals His divine purpose for our lives therefore it must be guarded from negativity, doubt, unbelief and all manner of impossibilities and presumptuous sins. The bible further encourages us in our pursuit, in our walk, to be totally sanctified. Here the words of the Savior in St. John 17:17, "Sanctify them through Thy truth: Thy word is truth."

At the altar of sanctification the word of God is to be used as a transport to bring us into a state of sanctification. Clearly it is virtually impossible to obtain/attain sanctification apart from the eternal Word. And not only that, at the altar of sanctification you will find in addition to the eternal Word, the eternal Spirit for they are in essence one and the same entity. This is what our Lord said: "the words that I speak unto you, they are spirit and they are life." St. John 6:63. It is the place where God encounters us and transforms our lives so that we would embrace the great commission and go out to affect change in the lives of others.

We have before us an extremely high calling from this altar of sanctification. As we bow in an attitude of humility, worship, honor and praise we lose our self worth and we present ourselves as that required offering and we become fully cognizant that we are in the presence of the Eternal Sovereign God of the universe and we cry out as Isaiah the prophet, "Woe is me for I am undone, because I am a man of unclean lips; and I dwell in the midst of a people with unclean lips: for mine eyes have seen the King, the Lord of hosts."

As we linger at this altar of sanctification we lose ourselves and become infused with the presence of a holy God. We lose all sense of time and place so much so that like Peter we find ourselves crying out, *"Lord it is good for us to be here, if thou wilt, let us make here three tabernacles; one for Thee, one for Moses and one for Elias."*

As we meditate on the awesome power and presence of God, we are moved to acknowledge the words of the inspired writer in the book of Hebrew, chapter 3, verses 1-2, where the apostle admonishes,

"wherefore, holy brethren, partakers of the heavenly calling, consider the Apostle and High Priest of our profession, *Christ Jesus; Who was faithful to him that appointed him, as also Moses was faithful in all his house."

And in chapter 4:1,

"Let us therefore fear, lest a promise being left us of entering into his rest, any of you should seem to come short of it."

With these strong words of admonition and consolation indeed, *"how shall we escape if we neglect so great salvation."*

My brother, my sister, let us draw nigh to God with a pure heart and a holy zeal to don on the wedding garment of sanctification. Matthew 22:11. This is a ticket to heaven purchased by the blood of the Lamb.

The Father assures us that we are *"engraved in the palms of His hands."* That is to say that the Lord's hands are not shortened that He cannot save, but that His hands are strong and that none can take out of the Father's hand. Isaiah 49:16.

It is important to remember that our God is well able to keep us from falling and to present us faultless/free from iniquity/ holy and sanctified before His throne of mercy. Jude 1:24-25.

Our God is well able to make us whole and complete in Christ, so that whatever our circumstances may be or may have been, whatever our conditions, present, past or future, whatever trauma, pain, sorrow, whatever abuse, whether as a victim or perpetrator, the provisions made for us on Calvary's cross is more than sufficient to make us sanctified vessels of the Most High God.

IX. The Altar of Sanctification

At the altar of sanctification you will find in addition to the eternal Word, the eternal Spirit for they are in essence one and the same entity.

About the Author
Dorothy V. McIntosh

Dorothy was born in Abaco, Bahamas; she is the ninth child in a family of 11 children. She is a woman of prayer who is used by God in areas of healing, deliverance and prophetic intercession. Her main objective is to establish a safe place for hurting women bringing healing and restoration to them.

She dedicates her time to prayer. She is a loving mother, grandmother, and friend. She is also an author, teacher, preacher, visionary, and prayer warrior, and songwriter. Dorothy has a deep love and passion for God and His work. She is an ordained Pastor, and Founder of "The Prayer Room Ministry," an Apostolic and Prophetic Prayer House, and CEO of "Apostolic Team Ministry" ATM.

YOU WRITE, WE PUBLISH, TOGETHER WE CREATE

DIVINE WORKS PUBLISHING, LLC.

A co-publishing service for indie authors seeking a strategic bigger partner alliance for greater visibility and success in today's overcrowded marketplace.

www.DivineWorksPublishing.com

561-990-BOOK (2665)

info@ DivineWorksPublishing.com

www.ingramcontent.com/pod-product-compliance
Lightning Source LLC
Chambersburg PA
CBHW030533080526
44586CB00011B/424